Oh! My Phonics

4

Double Letters

CEDU BOOK

INTRODUCTION

• WORD CHANT

The fun chants and captivating illustrations introduce the target sounds and words.

• LISTEN & REPEAT

Students can learn and practice the target sounds and words. They can also understand the letter-sound relationships.

• WORD READING

Students can practice reading words with the target sounds.

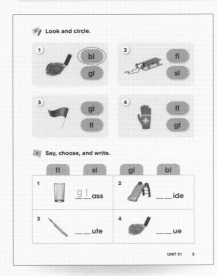

• WRITING

The target sounds and words can be strengthened through writing activities.

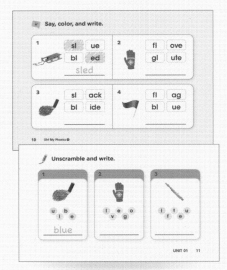

• LISTENING

Students can reinforce the target sounds and words through listening activities.

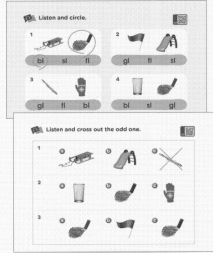

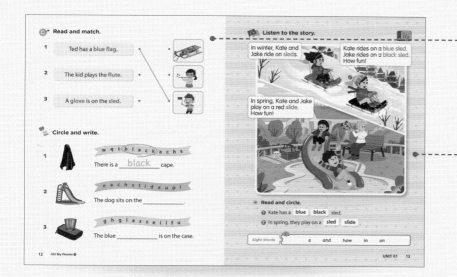

• SENTENCE READING

Students can practice reading sentences with the target words.

• STORY READING

A phonics story offers students practice with reading target words in natural contexts. They can naturally improve their sight word reading skills.

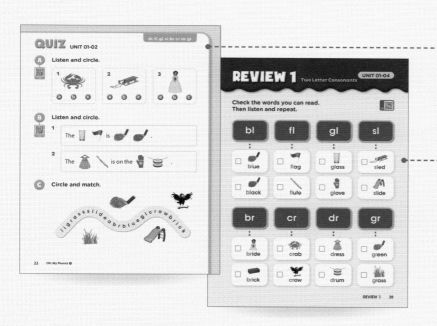

• UNIT QUIZ

Students can check what they have learned in the previous two units.

• REVIEW

A variety of activities can help students recall and further practice the sounds and words from previous units.

WORKBOOK

Students can reinforce what they have learned by completing the follow-up exercises featured in the accompanying workbook.

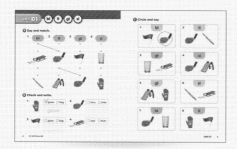

CONTENTS

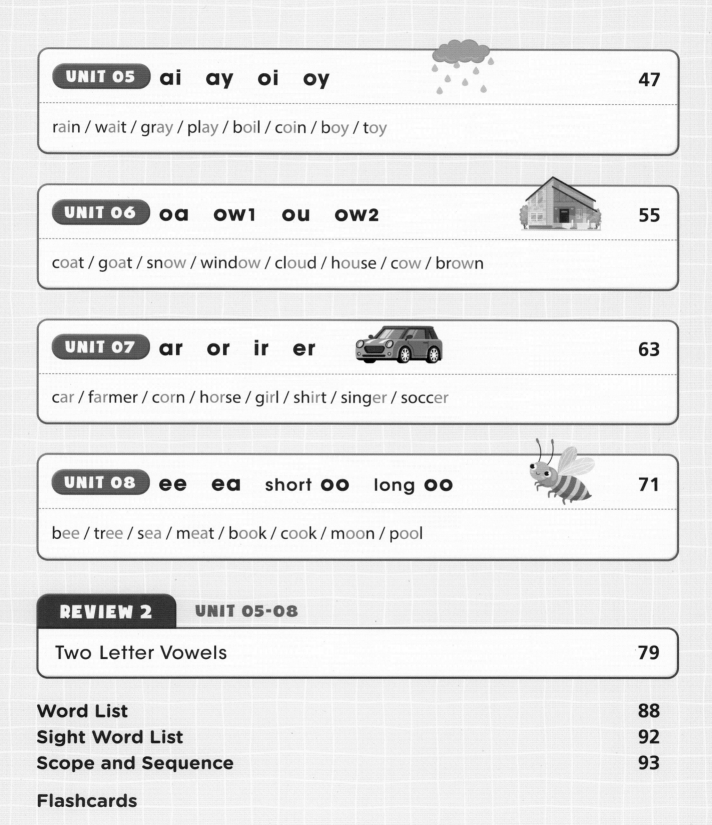

blue   black

flag   flute

glass   glove

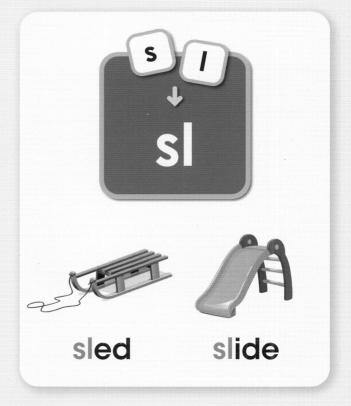

sled   slide

Look and circle.

1

bl

gl

2
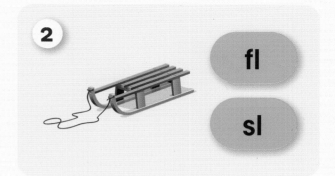
fl

sl

3
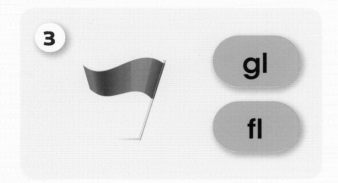
gl

fl

4

fl

gl

 Say, choose, and write.

fl   sl   gl   bl

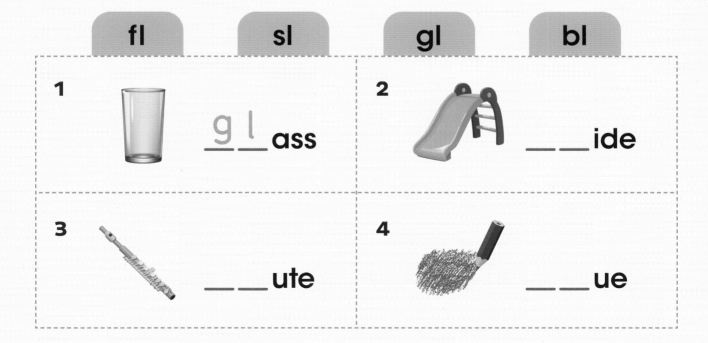

1 g l ass

2 ___ide

3 ___ute

4 ___ue

Listen and circle.

1
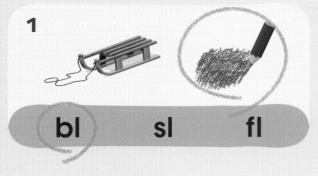

bl   sl   fl

2
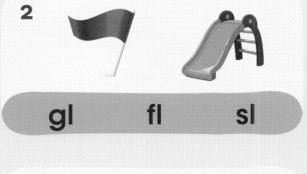

gl   fl   sl

3
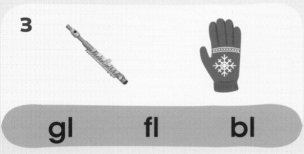

gl   fl   bl

4

bl   sl   gl

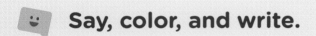 **Say, color, and write.**

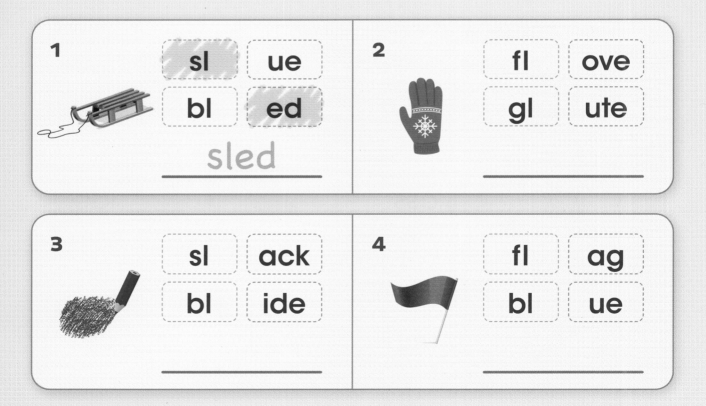

1

sl   ue
bl   ed

sled
_____

2

fl   ove
gl   ute

_____

3

sl   ack
bl   ide

_____

4

fl   ag
bl   ue

_____

Listen and cross out the odd one.

1 a b c

2 a b c

3 a b c

 # Unscramble and write.

1

u b l e

blue

2

l e o v g

_____

3

l t u f e

_____

Read and match.

1 Ted has a **blue flag**.

2 The kid plays the **flute**.

3 A **glove** is on the **sled**.

 Circle and write.

1

w q t b l a c k a c h s

There is a ___black___ cape.

2

e a c h s l i d e u p i

The dog sits on the _____.

3

g h g l a s s e i l f u

The blue _____ is on the case.

Listen to the story.

In winter, Kate and Jake ride on sleds.

Kate rides on a blue sled. Jake rides on a black sled. How fun!

In spring, Kate and Jake play on a red slide. How fun!

☀ **Read and circle.**

1 Kate has a blue   black sled.

2 In spring, they play on a sled   slide .

Sight Words   a   and   how   in   on

QUIZ UNIT 01

A Listen and circle.

06

1
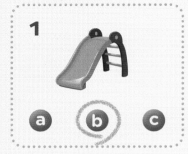
ⓐ ⓑ ⓒ

2
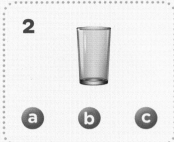
ⓐ ⓑ ⓒ

3
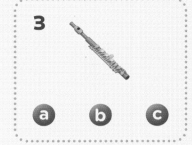
ⓐ ⓑ ⓒ

B Listen and circle.

07

1
The [sled] [flag] is under the slide.

2
I ride a [blue] [blue] bike.

C Circle and match.

mliflagblueabgloverblaceesrsled

Listen and chant.

bride

dress

crab

crow

drum

green

brick

grass

bride   brick

crab   crow

dress   drum

green   grass

Look and circle.

1
br
dr

2
cr
gr

3
dr
cr

4
br
cr

 **Say, choose, and write.**

cr   gr   dr   br

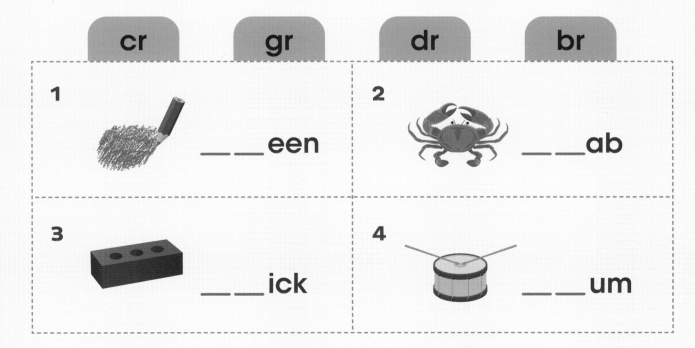

1 ___ ___een

2 ___ ___ab

3 ___ ___ick

4 ___ ___um

Listen and circle.

1

br   gr   cr

2

gr   dr   br

3

cr   dr   gr

4

br   dr   cr

 **Say, color, and write.**

1

gr   ide

br   ass

_____

2

dr   ab

cr   ess

_____

3

gr   um

dr   een

_____

4

br   ow

cr   ide

_____

Listen and cross out the odd one.

1   a   b   c

2   a   b   c

3   a   b   c

 ## Unscramble and write.

1

r o w c

_____

2

n r e e g

_____

3

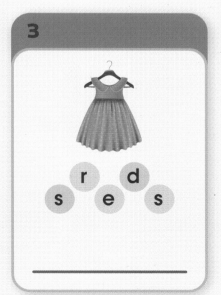

r d s e s

_____

Read and match.

1 Kate has **green** gloves. •

2 The **bride** plays the **drums**. •

3 The **crab** is on the **brick**. •

 Circle and write.

1

f h e i l d r e s s l w

The blue _____ is on the bed.

2

d r a e h g r a s s e i

The crow is on the _____.

3

s e a c r a b s l u e i

The cat has a _____ hat.

Listen to the story.

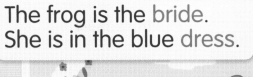
The frog is the bride.
She is in the blue dress.

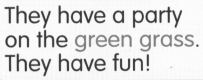
The crab plays the drums.
The crow plays the flute.

They have a party
on the green grass.
They have fun!

☀ **Read and circle.**

1 The bride's dress is green blue .

2 The crab crow plays the flute.

Sight Words | a have in is on plays she the they

A Listen and circle.

1  ⓐ ⓑ ⓒ

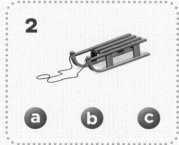

2 ⓐ ⓑ ⓒ

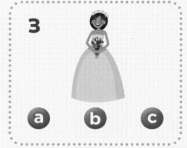

3 ⓐ ⓑ ⓒ

B Listen and circle.

1

The [ ] [ ] is [ ] [ ] .

2
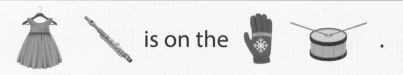

The [ ] [ ] is on the [ ] [ ] .

C Circle and match.

l i g r a s s s l i d e a b r b l u e g l c r o w b r c i y

UNIT 03

sm **sn** **st** **sw**

Two Letter Consonants

- Listen and chant.

15

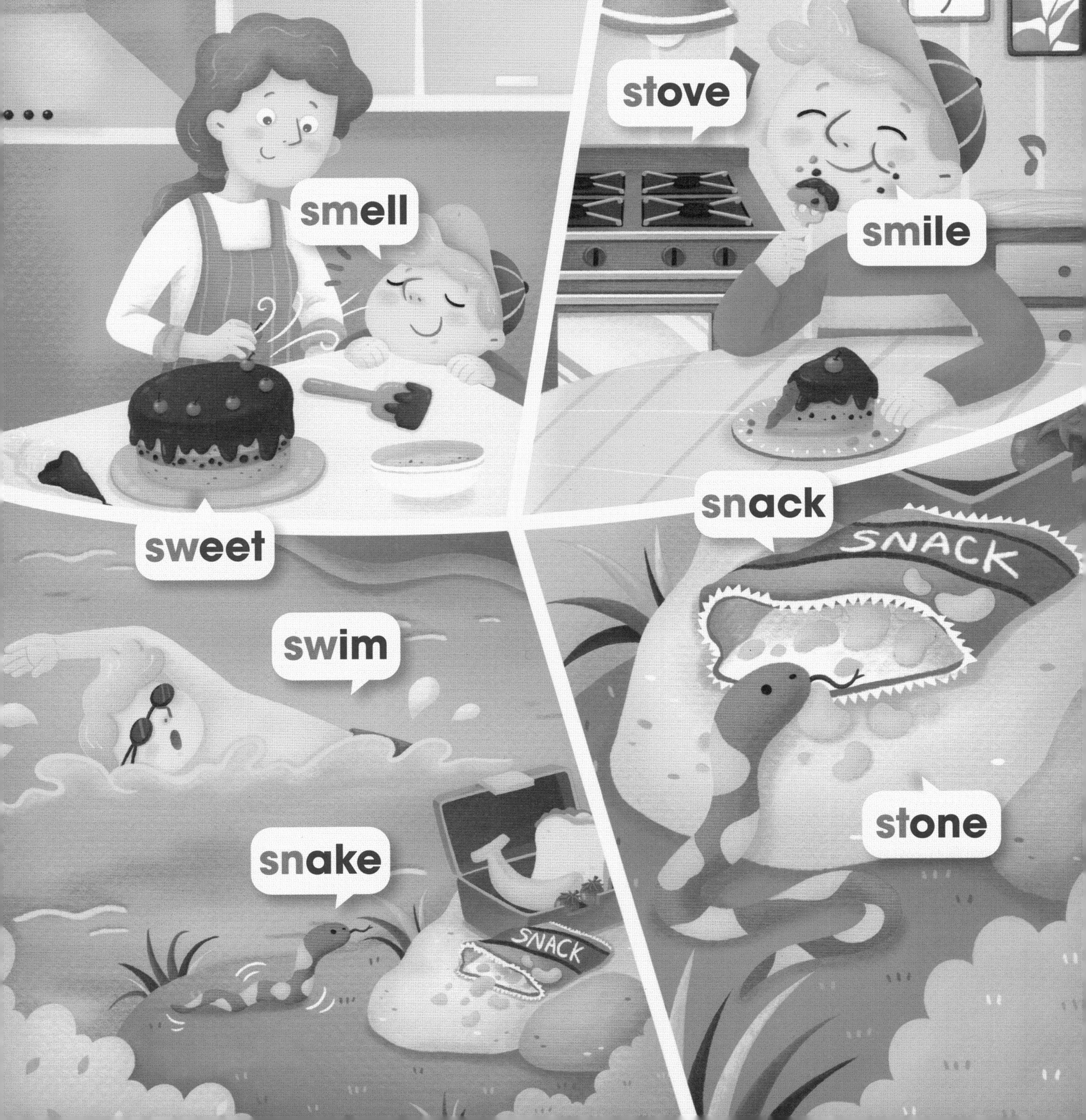
stove
smell
smile
sweet
snack
SNACK
swim
stone
snake
SNACK

smell   **smile**

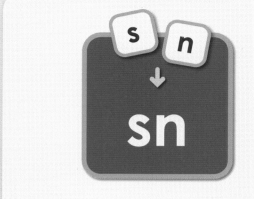

snake   **snack**

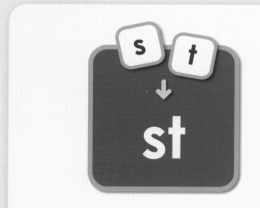

stone   **stove**

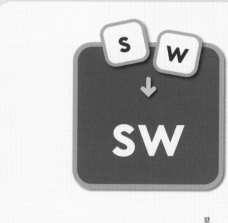

swim   **sweet**

Say and match.

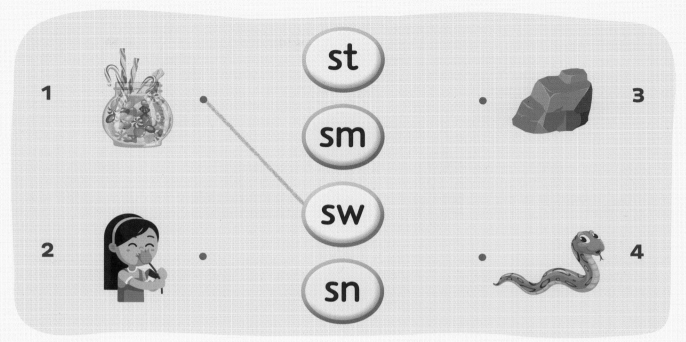

1   st   3

   sm

   sw

2   sn   4

 Say, choose, and write.

| sm | sn | st | sw |

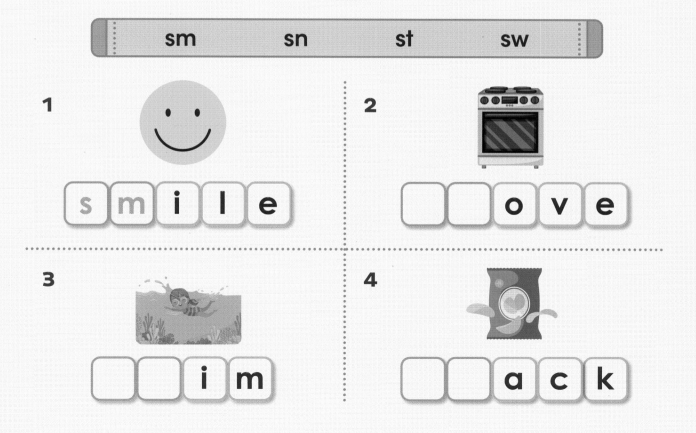

1   s m i l e

2   _ _ o v e

3   _ _ i m

4   _ _ a c k

Listen and circle.

1

sm   sn   sw   st

2

st   sn   sm   sw

Find, circle, and write.

1

2

3

4

s	n	q	e	s	e
z	m	l	a	n	d
k	n	i	y	a	f
s	t	e	l	k	g
j	s	w	e	e	t
s	t	o	v	e	a

1   sweet

2   _____

3   _____

4   _____

Listen and cross out the odd one.

✏ **Unscramble and write.**

1

i m
s w

_____

2

o n e
t s

_____

3

m e l
l s

_____

Read and match.

1   The pup **smells** the **snack**.   •

2   He likes the **sweet** cake.   •

3   The **snake** is on the **stone**.   •

 Circle and write.

1

u h e s m i l e w e r g

The kid has a cute _____.

2

d r u t s n l s w i m k

We _____ in the lake.

3

r v n s t o v e y s w b

The pot is on the _____.

Listen to the story.

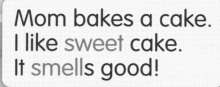

☀ **Read and circle.**

❶ The boy eats the [swim / sweet] cake.

❷ The snake smells the [cake / snack].

Sight Words	a	and	at	eat	good	he	I	in
	it	like	my	no	oh	see	the	

QUIZ UNIT 02-03

A Listen and circle.

20

1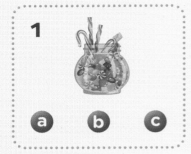

ⓐ ⓑ ⓒ

2

ⓐ ⓑ ⓒ

3

ⓐ ⓑ ⓒ

B Listen and circle.

21

1 There is a [image] [image] on the [image] [image] .

2 The cats [image] [image] the [image] [image] .

C Circle and match.

shop   fi**sh**

cherry   lun**ch**

three   mou**th**

si**ng**   ri**ng**

Say and match.

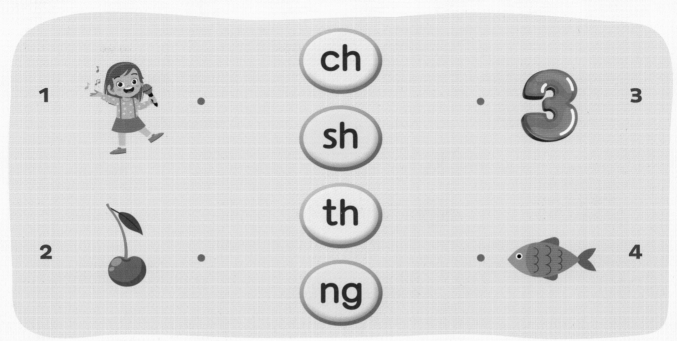

1 •   ch   • 3

          sh

          th

2 •   ng   • 4

 Say, choose, and write.

| sh | ng | ch | th |

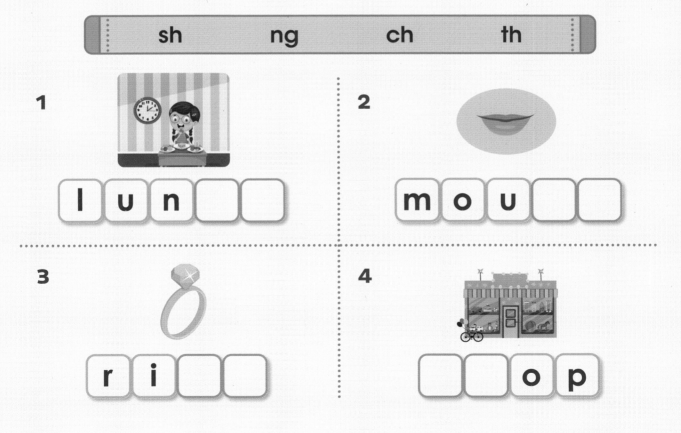

1 l u n ☐ ☐

2 m o u ☐ ☐

3 r i ☐ ☐

4 ☐ ☐ o p

Listen and circle.

1

ng   sh   th   ch

2

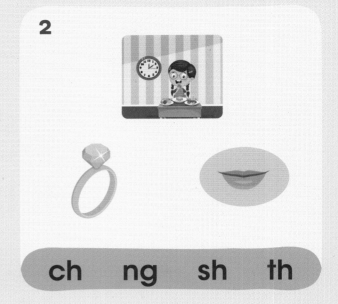

ch   ng   sh   th

 Find, circle, and write.

1    **2**

3   **4**

s	t	h	r	e	e
l	s	i	n	g	x
m	u	f	e	s	f
g	t	n	i	e	i
l	h	r	c	d	s
t	h	t	k	h	h

1 _____

2 _____

3 _____

4 _____

Listen and cross out the odd one.

1
- a
- b
- c

2
- a
- b
- c

3
- a
- b
- c

 Unscramble and write.

1

o p
h s

_____

2

i r
n g

_____

3

u m o
h t

_____

Read and match.

1 Three rings are in the case. •

2 The cherry jam is in the shop. •

3 Mom cooks the fish for lunch. •

 Circle and write.

1

q r s i n g e a s h k l

The man _____ s on the bed.

2

a t y u m o u t h p t h

The dog has a bone in its _____.

3

s k c h e r f i s h b g

The cats catch the _____.

Ted bakes cherry cupcakes for Kate.

It is Kate's birthday.
Ted and Glen have lunch and think.

Let's have a party!
Kate cooks fish.
Ted and Glen sing!

At the shop, Glen gets a ring for Kate.

✴ **Read and circle.**

❶ Ted bakes [fish] [cherry] cupcakes.

❷ Ted and Glen [ring] [sing] for Kate.

Sight Words	a	and	at	for	gets	have
	is	it	let's	the	think	

QUIZ UNIT 03-04

A Listen and circle.

1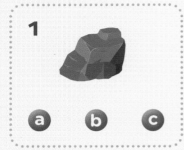

   a   **b**   **c**

2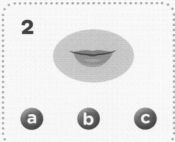

   a   **b**   **c**

3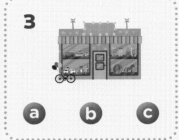

   a   **b**   **c**

B Listen and circle.

1

2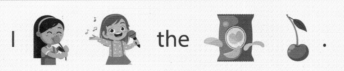

C Circle and match.

n c s w s n a k e l i u t h r i n g s t o v e l u n c h c v a

REVIEW 1

Two Letter Consonants

Check the words you can read.
Then listen and repeat.

bl	fl	gl	sl
☐ blue	☐ flag	☐ glass	☐ sled
☐ black	☐ flute	☐ glove	☐ slide

br	cr	dr	gr
☐ bride	☐ crab	☐ dress	☐ green
☐ brick	☐ crow	☐ drum	☐ grass

Check the words you can read.
Then listen and repeat.

sm
- ☐ smell
- ☐ smile

sn
- ☐ snake
- ☐ snack

st
- ☐ stone
- ☐ stove

sw
- ☐ swim
- ☐ sweet

sh
- ☐ shop
- ☐ fish

ch
- ☐ cherry
- ☐ lunch

th
- ☐ three
- ☐ mouth

ng
- ☐ sing
- ☐ ring

A Listen and circle.

1. glove (black)
2. snack swim
3. bride green
4. shop three

B Match and write.

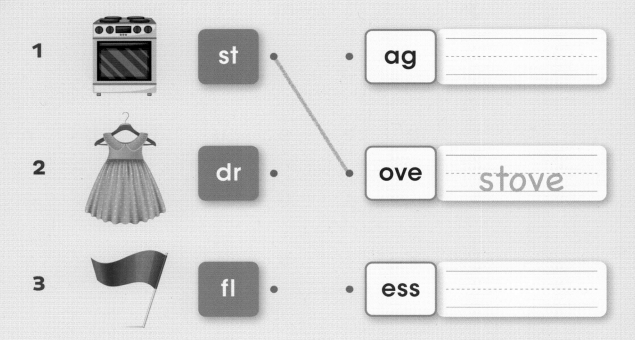

1. st — ag
2. dr — ove stove
3. fl — ess

C Find and circle.

r	d	c	l	u	n	c	h
i	g	r	a	s	s	t	s
n	c	s	w	e	e	t	h
g	r	f	m	t	w	y	e
e	a	a	l	e	q	d	u
s	b	e	e	u	l	b	n
s	l	i	d	e	t	l	s
j	k	j	b	l	n	e	v

D **Listen and check.**

32

1

2

3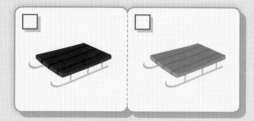

4

E **Listen and circle.**

33

1 The bride has a blue  .

2 The big pot is on the  .

3 A 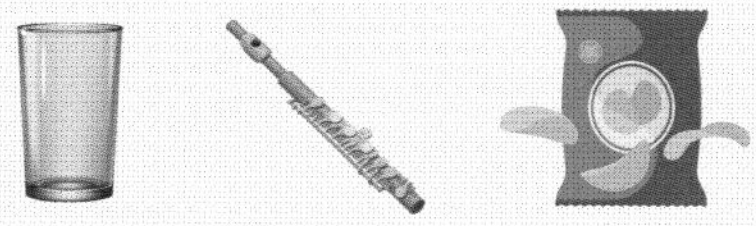 is in the box.

Look at the pictures and follow. Then write.

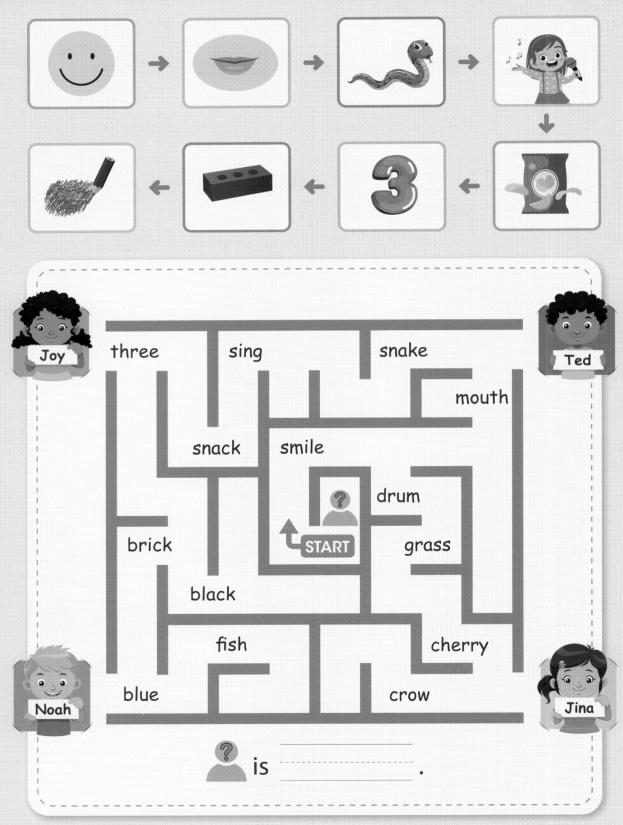

Joy three sing snake
Ted mouth
snack smile
drum
brick grass
START
black
fish cherry
blue crow
Noah
Jina

? is _____ .

G Find the words with the same two letters and write the numbers.

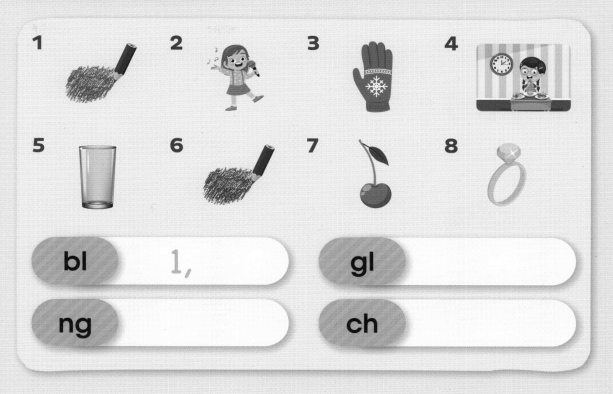

bl   1,

gl

ng

ch

H Which one has a different sound? Find and cross out.

1   cr

2   st

3   sh

Look, choose, and write.

1

blue   (flute)   black

They play the ___flute___ and drum.

2

sled   glove   smile

The boy has a cute _____.

3

mouth   snake   ring

It has a big _____.

4

stove   snack   grass

The ram is on the _____.

5

crow   crab   fish

The red _____ is on the tube.

• Listen and chant.

rain   wait

gray   play

boil   coin

boy   toy

Look and circle.

1  ai / oi

2  oy / ay

3  ai / oy

4  ay / ai

Say, choose, and write.

ay   oy   oi   ai

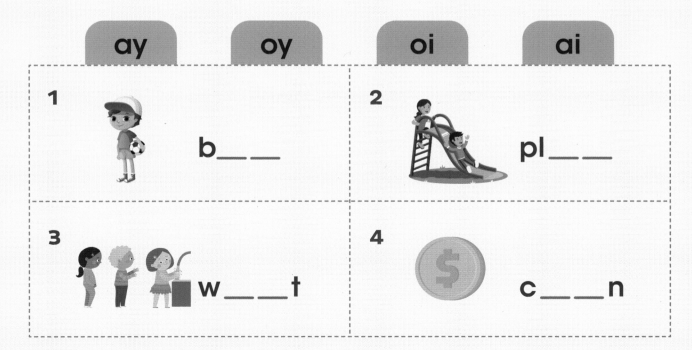

1 b_____

2 pl_____

3 w_____t

4 c_____n

Listen and circle.

1
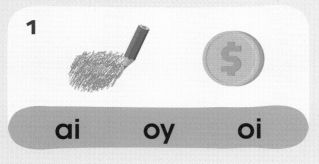

ai   oy   oi

2

ay   oi   ai

3

oi   oy   ai

4

ay   oy   ai

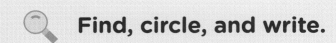 **Find, circle, and write.**

1 _____

2 _____

d k e w o b h b o y a i t
o c e z w n r a i n o v x
p l b o i l q a f g r a y

3 _____

4 _____

Listen and cross out the odd one.

1 a b c

2 a b c

3 a b c

 Unscramble and write.

1	2	3
	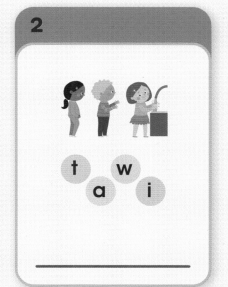	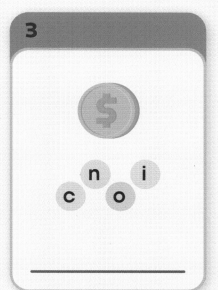
o t y	t w a i	n i c o
_____	_____	_____

Read and match.

1 The **boys play** on the grass. •

2 The man **waits** for **rain**. •

3 Gold **coin**s are in the box. •

 Circle and write.

1

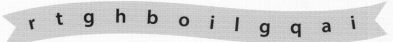
r t g h b o i l g q a i

The water _____ s on the stove.

2

d r a e h b m g r a y o

The elephant is big and _____.

3

p o k d g t o y t a w v

The boy is in the _____ shop.

Listen to the story.

It is raining and the sky is gray.

It is cold today. Mom boils water for tea.

I play with toys and coins at home. It's not fun.

Rain, stop! I want to play in the park. I wait and wait.

☀ **Read and circle.**

❶ The sky is gray coin .

❷ The boy wants to play wait in the park.

Sight Words

and at for I in is it it's
not sky stop the to want with

QUIZ UNIT 04-05

A Listen and circle.

1
ⓐ   ⓑ   ⓒ

2
ⓐ   ⓑ   ⓒ

3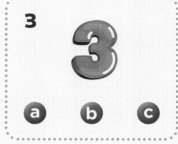
ⓐ   ⓑ   ⓒ

B Listen and circle.

1 The 🏪 🧒 has a 🕐🧒 🖌 bag.

2 The kids 🛝 🎶 with a 🌧 🐴 .

C Circle and match.

oa OW1 ou OW2

Two Letter Vowels

● Listen and chant.

coat   goat

snow   window

cloud   house

cow   brown

Look and circle.

1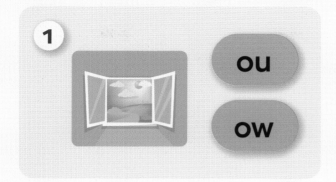
ou
ow

2
ou
ow

3
oa
ow

4
ou
oa

Say, choose, and write.

ou   ow   oa

1 sn___

2 h___se

3 g___t

4 c___

Listen and circle.

1

ow   ou   oa

2

ou   oa   ow

3

ou   oa   ow

4

oa   ow   ou

 Find, circle, and write.

1 _____

2 _____

c h e w i n d o w y a b t
o c c o w n r h o u s e q
l s b d o g o a t f g r k

3  _____

4 _____

Listen and cross out the odd one.

1 a   b   c

2 a   b   c

3 a   b   c

 **Unscramble and write.**

1

w s
o n

_____

2

l u o
d   c

_____

3

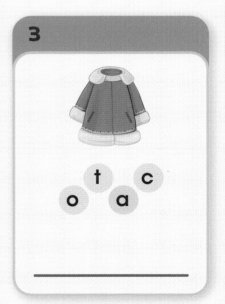

t   c
o a

_____

Read and match.

1 I like my **brown coat**. •

2 The **house** has many **windows**. •

3 There are three black **goats**. •

 Circle and write.

1

g h c i c o w n t j m a

The _____ is in the hut.

2

u i h j c l o u d f v b

I see a big gray _____.

3

o j c x f g q w s n o w

The kids play in the _____.

Listen to the story.

This is my house.
We have a cow and a goat.

The cow is brown
and the goat is black.

It's snowy today!
I play in the snow.

Where are the cow
and the goat?
Oh, they are in the
snow!

☀ **Read and circle.**

❶ There is a brown goat cow .

❷ The girl plays in the house snow .

Sight Words

a	and	are	have	I	in	is	it's
my	oh	the	they	this	we	where	

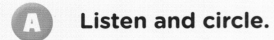
QUIZ UNIT 05-06

A Listen and circle.

1
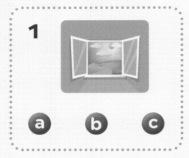
(a) (b) (c)

2
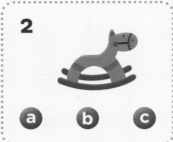
(a) (b) (c)

3
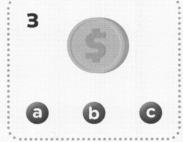
(a) (b) (c)

B Listen and circle.

1

The boy likes the  .

2

The pig plays with the  .

C Circle and match.

• Listen and chant.

car

girl

Jen

soccer

Ted

singer

shirt

Sam

horse

corn

farmer

Wendy

car   **farmer**

corn   **horse**

girl   **shirt**

singer   **soccer**

Say and match.

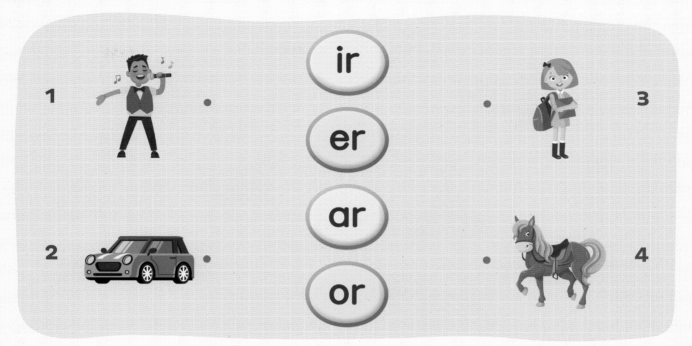

1

2

ir

er

ar

or

3

4

 Say, choose, and write.

| or | er | ar | ir |

1

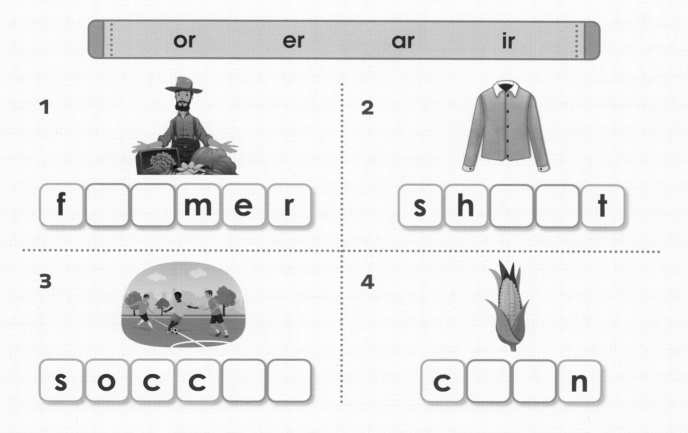

f [ ] [ ] m e r

2

s h [ ] [ ] t

3

s o c c [ ] [ ]

4

c [ ] [ ] n

Listen and circle.

1

or   er   ar

2

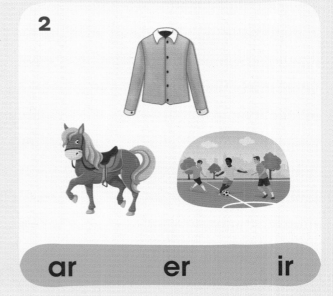

ar   er   ir

Find, circle, and write.

1

2

3

4

s	g	o	u	t	h
l	i	n	c	a	r
t	r	n	k	S	g
g	l	r	g	e	n
t	t	r	e	e	i
h	o	r	s	e	r

1 _____

2 _____

3 _____

4 _____

Listen and cross out the odd one.

51

1   a   b   c

2   a   b   c

3   a   b   c

Unscramble and write.

1	2	3
	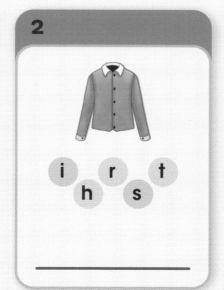	
r n o c	i r t h s	s c o e r c
_____	_____	_____

Read and match.

1 The **girls** play **soccer**. •   •

2 The **farmer** has five **horses**. •   •

3 The **singer** has a blue **shirt**. •   •

 Circle and write.

1

s h c a r g j k v n m d

The man has a red _____.

2

f g l o q w h o r s e s

The girl rides a _____.

3

c n v b s x s i n g e r

The _____ sings in the park.

Listen to the story.

※ **Read and circle.**

1 Ted wants to be a [soccer | singer] player.

2 Wendy likes [car | corn] and horses.

Sight Words	a and be I like to want

QUIZ UNIT 06-07

A Listen and circle.

1	2	3
	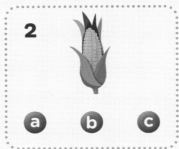	
a b c	a b c	a b c

B Listen and circle.

1 The brown  is in the  .

2 A  and a  are in the farm.

C Circle and match.

• Listen and chant.

55

book

sea

bee

tree

cook

meat

pool

moon

bee　　**tree**

sea　　**meat**

book　　**cook**

moon　　**pool**

Say and match.

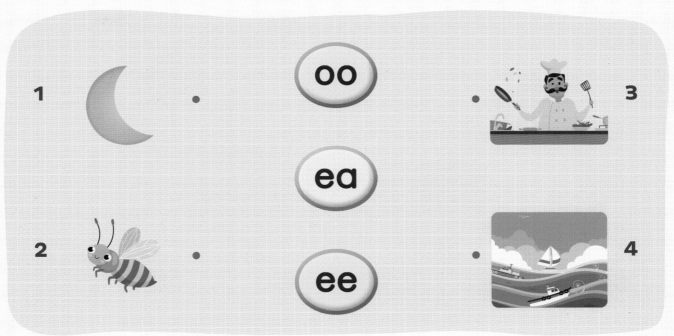

1   🌙

oo

ea

2   🐝

ee

3

4

Say, choose, and write.

| ea | oo | ee |

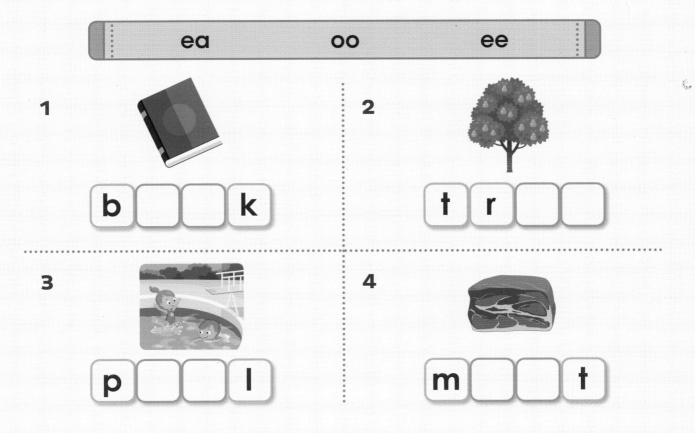

1   b [ ] [ ] k

2   t r [ ] [ ]

3   p [ ] [ ] l

4   m [ ] [ ] t

Listen and circle.

1

ea   oo   ee

2

oo   ea   ee

 Find, circle, and write.

1

2

3

4

g	u	s	e	a	o
l	i	m	c	t	x
t	r	o	b	e	g
g	l	o	o	e	n
t	f	n	o	f	e
c	o	o	k	e	r

1 _____

2 _____

3 _____

4 _____

Listen and cross out the odd one.

1 a   b   c

2 a   b   c

3 a   b   c

 ## Unscramble and write.

1

o k
b o

_____

2

a e
t m

_____

3

l p
o o

_____

Read and match.

1 The kids swim in the **pool**. •

2 A **bee** sits on the **book**. •

3 The man **cooks** the **meat**. •

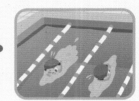

 Circle and write.

1

s g h w e d f g s e a k

I swim in the blue _____.

2

w b t r e e j h d s a s

A bear sleeps under the _____.

3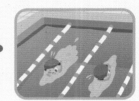

q x v b j d a g m o o n

I see the _____ in the sky.

Listen to the story.

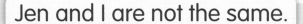

Jen and I are not the same.

She likes green trees.

She likes to read a book.

She likes to swim in the sea.

What do I like?

I like to swim in the pool.

I like to cook.

I like the moon.

✴ **Read and circle.**

❶ Jen likes green trees. Yes No

❷ Jen and I like to cook. Yes No

Sight Words a and are do I like likes not she the to what

UNIT 07-08

A Listen and circle.

1	2	3
	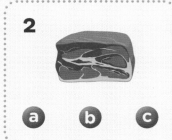	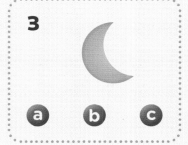
ⓐ ⓑ ⓒ	ⓐ ⓑ ⓒ	ⓐ ⓑ ⓒ

B Listen and circle.

1

The  has a  .

2

The  is under the   .

C Circle and match.

heyfarmerlukpoolascornqcvbee

Check the words you can read.
Then listen and repeat.

ai	**ay**	**oi**	**oy**
☐ rain	☐ gray	☐ boil	☐ boy
☐ wait	☐ play	☐ coin	☐ toy

oa	**ow1**	**ou**	**ow2**
☐ coat	☐ snow	☐ cloud	☐ cow
☐ goat	☐ window	☐ house	☐ brown

Check the words you can read.
Then listen and repeat.

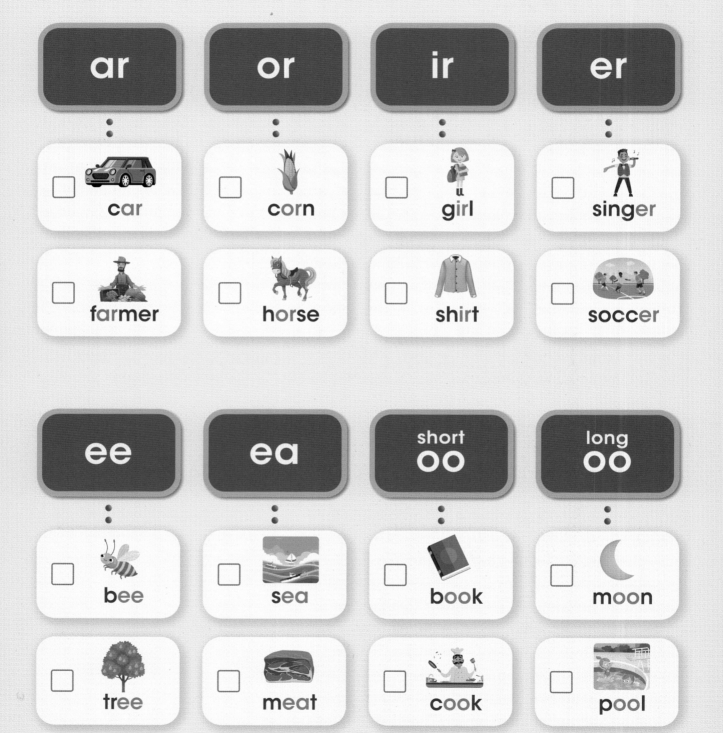

ar	or	ir	er
car	corn	girl	singer
farmer	horse	shirt	soccer

ee	ea	short **oo**	long **oo**
bee	sea	book	moon
tree	meat	cook	pool

A Listen and cirlce.

1

(coin)   rain

2

boy   gray

3

book   moon

4

farmer   singer

B Match and write.

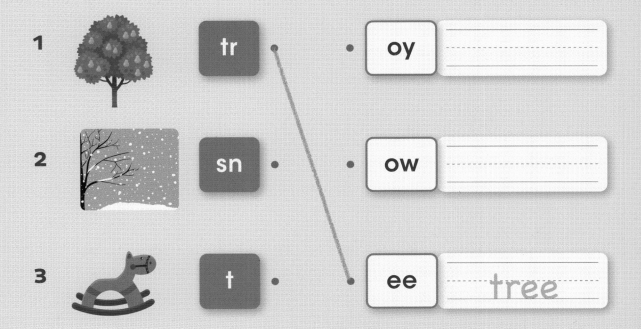

1   tr •   • oy _____

2   sn •   • ow _____

3   t •   • ee _tree_____

g	h	c	o	r	n	p	d
l	a	o	l	p	r	l	a
g	o	a	t	o	n	a	r
p	a	f	m	t	u	y	e
o	m	a	o	j	q	d	c
o	g	i	r	l	i	b	f
l	i	s	i	n	g	e	r
u	k	x	b	r	o	w	n

D Listen and check.

1

2

3

4

E Listen and circle.

1 The  plays in the   .

2 The 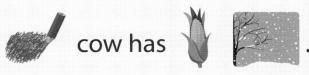 cow has .

3 The  cooks a big 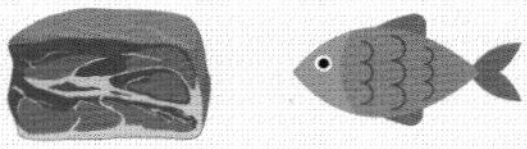 .

F Look at the pictures and follow. Then write.

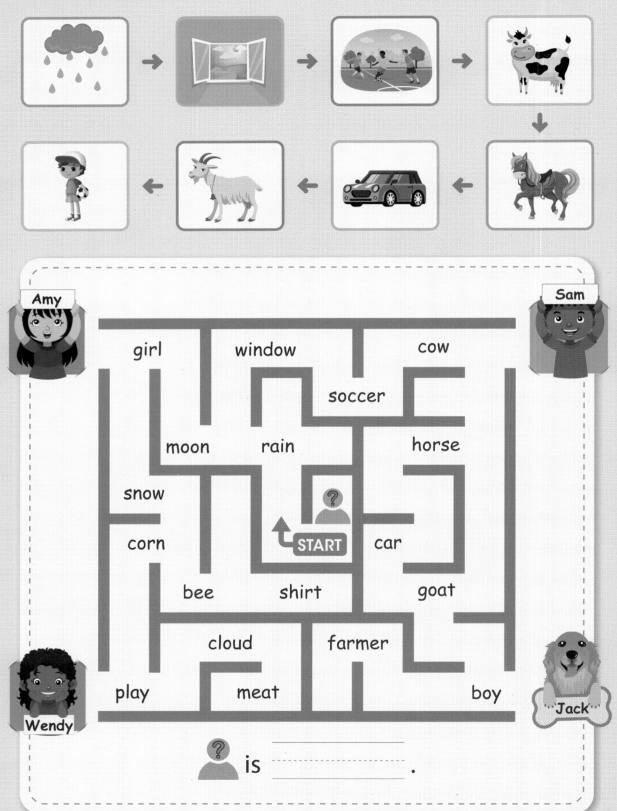

rain → window → soccer → cow → horse → car → goat → boy

? is _____ .

G Find the words with the same two letters and write the numbers.

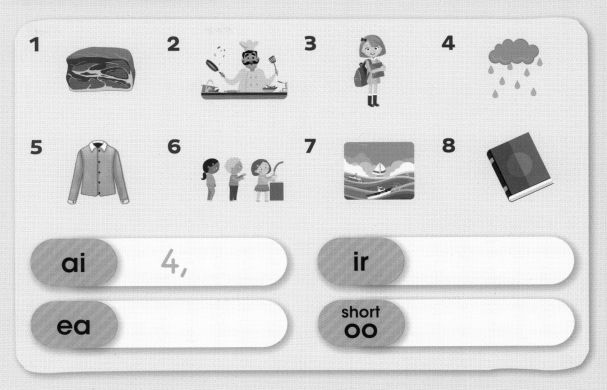

| ai | 4, | | ir | |
| ea | | | short **oo** | |

H Which one has a different sound? Find and cross out.

I Look, choose, and write.

1

rain	snow	cloud

The dogs run in the _____rain_____.

2

girl	tree	window

The _____s are red and yellow.

3

book	shirt	toy

The boy buys a _____ at the shop.

4

soccer	cook	singer

Dad likes to play _____.

5

coin	wait	boil

The man _____s water in a pot.

WORD LIST

• Can you read? Read and check.

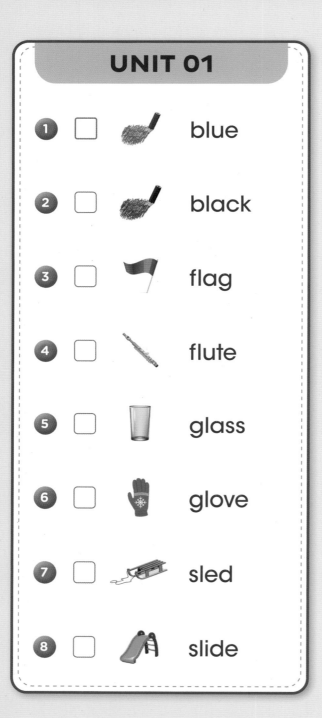

UNIT 01

1. ☐ blue
2. ☐ black
3. ☐ flag
4. ☐ flute
5. ☐ glass
6. ☐ glove
7. ☐ sled
8. ☐ slide

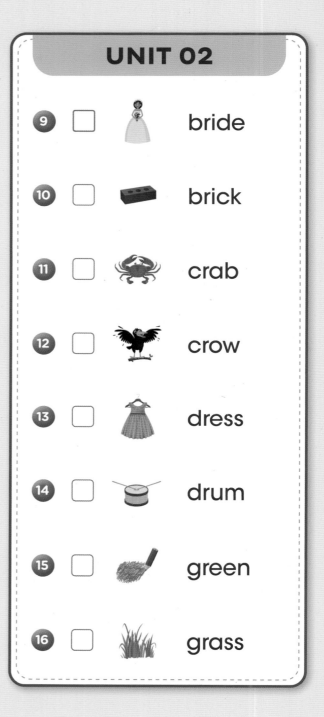

UNIT 02

9. ☐ bride
10. ☐ brick
11. ☐ crab
12. ☐ crow
13. ☐ dress
14. ☐ drum
15. ☐ green
16. ☐ grass

UNIT 03

17 ☐ 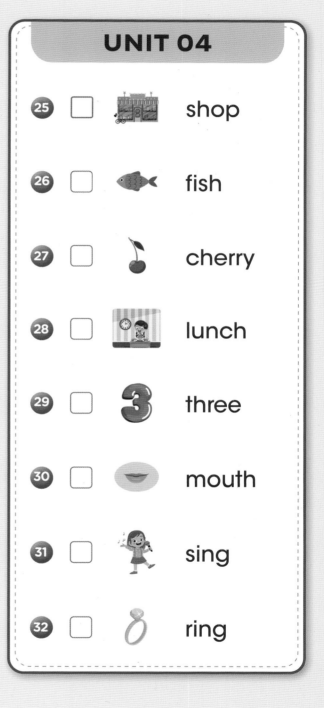 smell

18 ☐ smile

19 ☐ snake

20 ☐ snack

21 ☐ stone

22 ☐ stove

23 ☐ swim

24 ☐ sweet

UNIT 04

25 ☐ shop

26 ☐ fish

27 ☐ cherry

28 ☐ lunch

29 ☐ three

30 ☐ mouth

31 ☐ sing

32 ☐ ring

WORD LIST

• Can you read? Read and check.

UNIT 05

33. ☐ rain
34. ☐ wait
35. ☐ gray
36. ☐ play
37. ☐ boil
38. ☐ coin
39. ☐ boy
40. ☐ toy

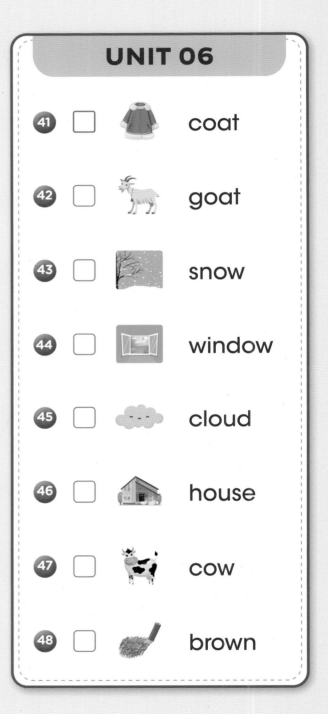

UNIT 06

41. ☐ coat
42. ☐ goat
43. ☐ snow
44. ☐ window
45. ☐ cloud
46. ☐ house
47. ☐ cow
48. ☐ brown

UNIT 07

49 ☐  car

50 ☐ farmer

51 ☐ corn

52 ☐ horse

53 ☐ girl

54 ☐ shirt

55 ☐ singer

56 ☐ soccer

UNIT 08

57 ☐ bee

58 ☐ tree

59 ☐ sea

60 ☐ meat

61 ☐ book

62 ☐ cook

63 ☐ moon

64 ☐ pool

SIGHT WORD LIST

• **Can you read? Read and check.**

#		Word	Numbers
1	☐	a	13, 21, 29, 37, 61, 69, 77
2	☐	and	13, 29, 37, 53, 61, 69, 77
3	☐	are	61, 77
4	☐	at	29, 37, 53
5	☐	be	69
6	☐	do	77
7	☐	eat	29
8	☐	for	37, 53
9	☐	gets	37
10	☐	good	29
11	☐	have	21, 37, 61
12	☐	he	29
13	☐	how	13
14	☐	I	29, 53, 61, 69, 77
15	☐	in	13, 21, 29, 53, 61
16	☐	is	21, 37, 53, 61
17	☐	it	29, 37, 53
18	☐	it's	53, 61
19	☐	let's	37
20	☐	like	29, 69, 77
21	☐	likes	77

#		Word	Numbers
22	☐	my	29, 61
23	☐	no	29
24	☐	not	53, 77
25	☐	oh	29, 61
26	☐	on	13, 21
27	☐	plays	21
28	☐	see	29
29	☐	she	21, 77
30	☐	sky	53
31	☐	stop	53
32	☐	the	21, 29, 37, 53, 61, 77
33	☐	they	21, 61
34	☐	think	37
35	☐	this	61
36	☐	to	53, 69, 77
37	☐	want	53, 69
38	☐	we	61
39	☐	what	77
40	☐	where	61
41	☐	with	53

SCOPE & SEQUENCE

Book 1 — Alphabet Sounds

UNIT 01	Aa Bb Cc
UNIT 02	Dd Ee Ff
UNIT 03	Gg Hh Ii
UNIT 04	Jj Kk Ll
UNIT 05	Mm Nn Oo
UNIT 06	Pp Qq Rr
UNIT 07	Ss Tt Uu Vv
UNIT 08	Ww Xx Yy Zz

Book 2 — Short Vowels

UNIT 01	Short Vowel a: am, ag, ap
UNIT 02	Short Vowel a: ad, an, at
UNIT 03	Short Vowel i: ig, in, ip
UNIT 04	Short Vowel i: id, it, ix
UNIT 05	Short Vowel e: ed, en, et
UNIT 06	Short Vowel o: og, ot, ox
UNIT 07	Short Vowel u: ug, un, up
UNIT 08	Short Vowel u: ub, ud, ut

Book 3 — Long Vowels

UNIT 01	Short Vowels Review
UNIT 02	Long Vowel a: a_e
UNIT 03	Long Vowel a: a_e
UNIT 04	Long Vowel i: i_e
UNIT 05	Long Vowel i: i_e
UNIT 06	Long Vowel o: o_e
UNIT 07	Long Vowel o: o_e
UNIT 08	Long Vowel u: u_e

Book 4 — Double Letters

UNIT 01	Consonant Blends : bl, fl, gl, sl
UNIT 02	Consonant Blends : br, cr, dr, gr
UNIT 03	Consonant Blends : sm, sn, st, sw
UNIT 04	Consonant Digraphs : sh, ch, th, ng
UNIT 05	Vowel Digraphs : ai, ay Vowel Diphthongs : oi, oy
UNIT 06	Vowel Digraphs : oa, ow1 (snow) Vowel Diphthongs : ou, ow2 (cow)
UNIT 07	R-controlled Vowels : ar, or, ir, er
UNIT 08	Vowel Digraphs: ee, ea, short oo, long oo

MEMO

MEMO

UNIT 01

UNIT 01

UNIT 01

UNIT 01

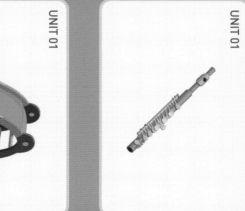

UNIT 01

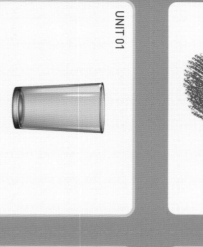

UNIT 01

UNIT 02

UNIT 02

UNIT 02

UNIT 02

UNIT 02

UNIT 02

UNIT 02

UNIT 02

UNIT 02

blue

glass

bride

dress

black

glove

brick

drum

flag

sled

crab

green

flute

slide

crow

grass

UNIT 04

UNIT 04

UNIT 04

UNIT 04

UNIT 04

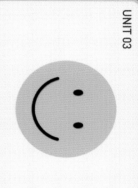

UNIT 04

UNIT 04

UNIT 04

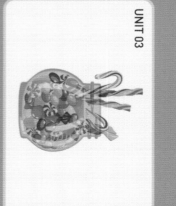

UNIT 03

UNIT 03

UNIT 03

UNIT 03

UNIT 03

UNIT 03

UNIT 03

snack

SAYPEN

snake

SAYPEN

smile

SAYPEN

smell

SAYPEN

sweet

SAYPEN

swim

SAYPEN

stove

SAYPEN

stone

SAYPEN

lunch

SAYPEN

cherry

SAYPEN

fish

SAYPEN

shop

SAYPEN

ring

SAYPEN

sing

SAYPEN

mouth

SAYPEN

three

SAYPEN

UNIT 05

UNIT 05

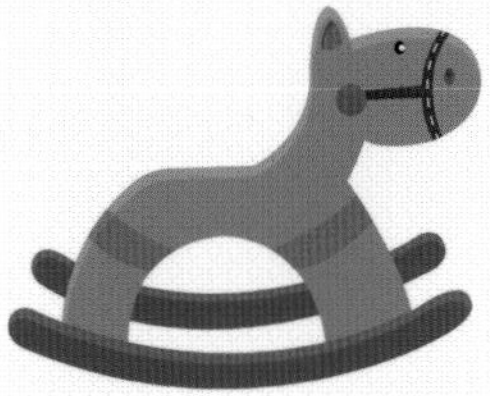

UNIT 06

UNIT 06

UNIT 05

UNIT 05

UNIT 06

UNIT 06

UNIT 05

UNIT 05

UNIT 06

UNIT 06

UNIT 05

UNIT 05

UNIT 06

UNIT 06

rain

wait

gray

play

boil

coin

boy

toy

coat

goat

snow

window

cloud

house

cow

brown

UNIT 07

UNIT 07

UNIT 08

UNIT 08

UNIT 07

UNIT 07

UNIT 08

UNIT 08

UNIT 07

UNIT 07

UNIT 08

UNIT 08

UNIT 07

UNIT 07

UNIT 08

UNIT 08

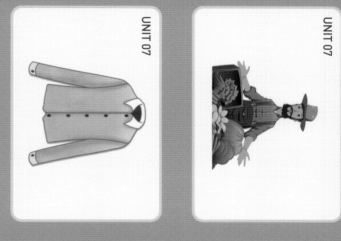

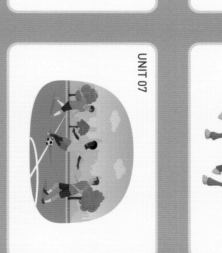
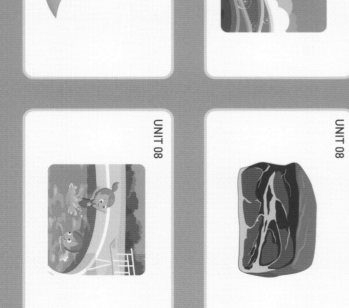

car	farmer	corn	horse
girl	shirt	singer	soccer
bee	tree	sea	meat
book	cook	moon	pool

with 세이펜

원어민 발음을 실시간 반복학습	단어 및 문장의 우리말 해석 듣기	발음을 듣고 따라 해보며 혼자서도 쉽게 학습

세이펜 핀파일 다운로드 안내

STEP ① 세이펜과 컴퓨터를 USB 케이블로 연결하세요.

STEP ② 쎄듀북 홈페이지(www.cedubook.com)에 접속 후, 학습자료실 메뉴에서 학습할 교재를 찾아 이동합니다.

> 초등교재 ▶ ELT ▶ 학습교재 클릭 ▶ 세이펜 핀파일 자료 클릭
> ▶ 다운로드 (저장을 '다른 이름으로 저장'으로 변경하여 저장소를 USB로 변경) ▶ 완료

STEP ③ 음원 다운로드가 완료되면 세이펜과 컴퓨터의 USB 케이블을 분리하세요.

STEP ④ 세이펜을 분리하면 "시스템을 초기화 중입니다. 잠시만 기다려 주세요."라는 멘트가 나옵니다.

STEP ⑤ 멘트 종료 후 세이펜을 〈Oh! My Phonics〉 표지에 대보세요.
효과음이 나온 후 바로 학습을 시작할 수 있습니다.

참고사항

◆ 세이펜은 본 교재에 포함되어 있지 않습니다. 별도로 구매하여 이용할 수 있으며, 기존에 보유하신 세이펜이 있다면 핀파일만 다운로드해서
바로 이용하실 수 있습니다.

◆ 세이펜에서 제작된 모든 기종(기존에 보유하고 계신 기종도 호환 가능)으로 사용이 가능합니다.

◆ 모든 기종은 세이펜에서 권장하는 최신 펌웨어 업데이트를 진행해 주시기 바랍니다.
업데이트는 세이펜 홈페이지(www.saypen.com)에서 가능합니다.

◆ 핀파일은 쎄듀북 홈페이지(www.cedubook.com)와 세이펜 홈페이지(www.saypen.com)에서 모두 다운로드 가능합니다.

◆ 세이펜을 이용하지 않는 학습자는 쎄듀북 홈페이지 부가학습자료, 교재 내 QR코드 이미지 등을 활용하여 원어민 음성으로 학습하실 수 있습니다.

◆ 기타 문의사항은 www.cedubook.com / 02-3272-4766으로 연락 바랍니다.

세이펜과 함께 배우는 Oh! My Phonics

〈Oh! My Phonics〉의 Student Book과 부록 플래시카드에는 세이펜이 적용되어 있습니다. 세이펜을 가져다 대기만 하면
원어민의 생생한 영어 발음과 억양을 듣고 영어 말하기 연습을 할 수 있습니다.

*번역 기능 | 세이펜으로 책을 찍어서 원어민 음성을 들은 후, T 버튼을 짧게 누르면 우리말 해석 음원을 들을 수 있습니다.

✏ 세이펜을 대면 Activity의 지시문을
들을 수 있습니다. T 기능 지원

✏ 유닛에서 배우게 될 글자에 세이펜을 대면
원어민의 정확한 발음을 들을 수 있습니다.

✏ QR코드에 세이펜을 대면
해당 트랙의 MP3 파일이
재생됩니다.

✏ 각 단어나 그림에 세이펜을
대면 원어민의 정확한 발음과
억양을 들을 수 있습니다.
T 기능 지원

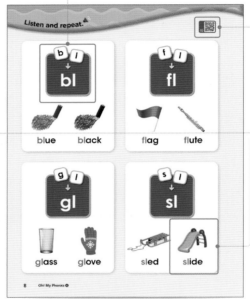

✏ 각 그림에 세이펜을 대면
원어민의 정확한 발음과
억양을 들을 수 있습니다.
T 기능 지원

✏ Listening 활동의 문제
번호에 펜을 대면 해당
문항의 음원이 재생됩니다.

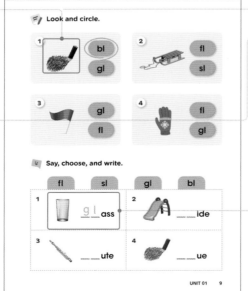

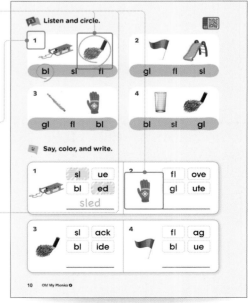

Oh! My Phonics

My

Phonics

4

Double Letters

Workbook

CEDU BOOK

Oh! My Phonics 4

Double Letters

Workbook

CEDUBOOK

CONTENTS

A Say and match.

1 bl   2 fl   3 gl   4 sl

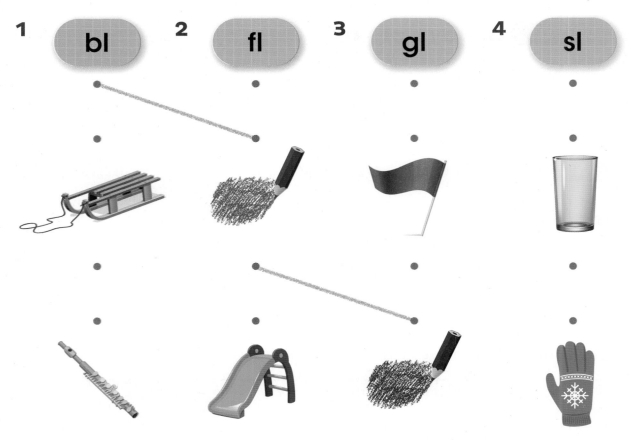

B Check and write.

1 ☑ glove ☐ flag

glove

2 ☐ blue ☐ slide

3 ☐ glass ☐ flag

4 ☐ sled ☐ flute

C Circle and say.

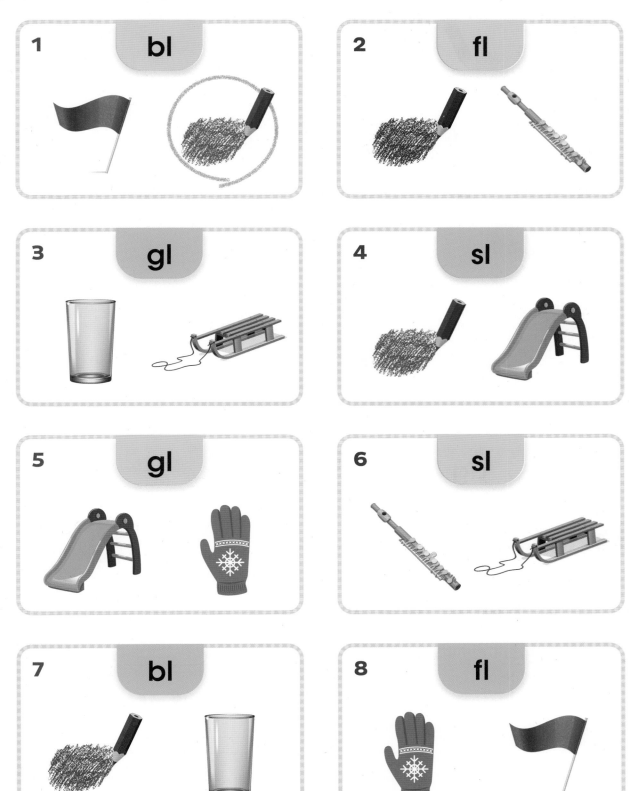

D Write the missing letters.

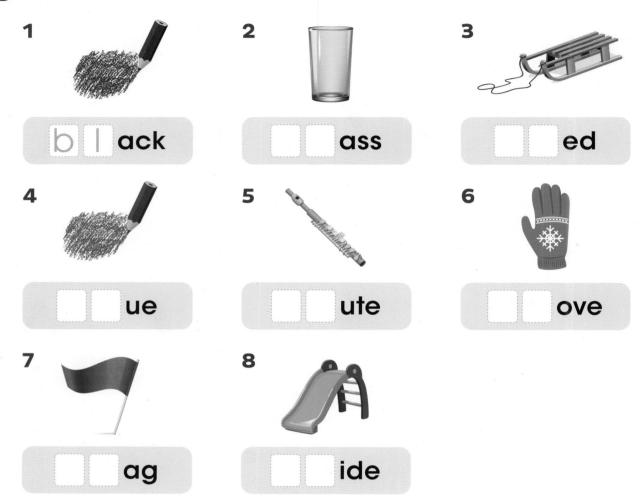

1 b l ack

2 □ □ ass

3 □ □ ed

4 □ □ ue

5 □ □ ute

6 □ □ ove

7 □ □ ag

8 □ □ ide

E Find and circle.

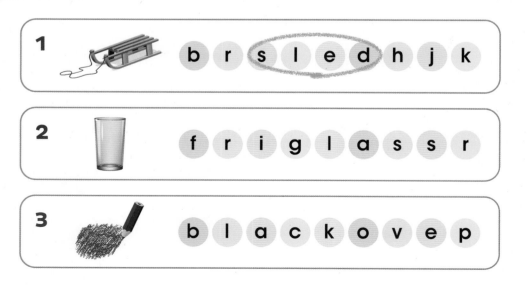

1 b r (s l e d) h j k

2 f r i g l a s s r

3 b l a c k o v e p

F Trace and write.

1  glove

2 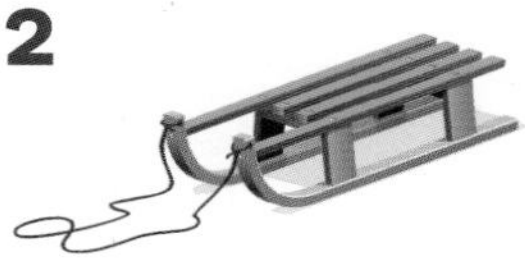 sled

3  black

4  blue

5 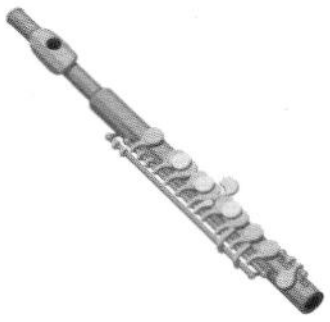 flute

6  slide

7  flag

8  glass

Ⓐ Say and match.

1 **gr**   2 **cr**   3 **dr**   4 **br**

Ⓑ Check and write.

1    ☐ brick ☐ crow

2    ☐ crab ☐ grass

3    ☐ dress ☐ green

4   ☐ bride ☐ drum

C Circle and say.

1 br

2 cr

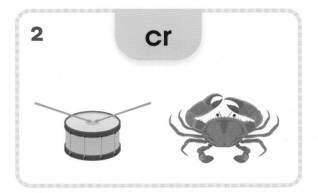

3 dr

4 gr

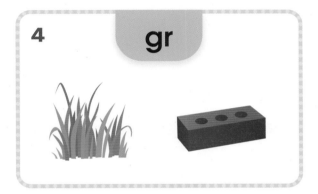

5 cr

6 dr

7 br

8 gr

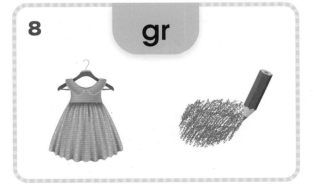

D Write the missing letters.

1 ☐☐ick

2 ☐☐ess

3 ☐☐een

4 ☐☐ide

5 ☐☐ab

6 ☐☐um

7 ☐☐ow

8 ☐☐ass

E Find and circle.

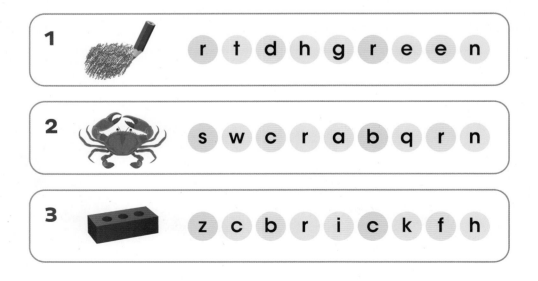

1 r t d h g r e e n

2 s w c r a b q r n

3 z c b r i c k f h

F **Trace and write.**

1  drum

2  green

3  brick

4  bride

5  crab

6  grass

7  crow

8  dress

A Say and match.

1 sw   **2** sn   **3** st   **4** sm

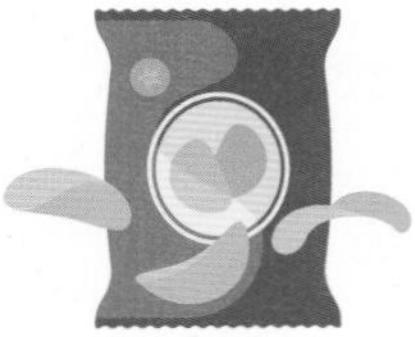

B Check and write.

1   ☐ stove ☐ snack

2   ☐ smell ☐ swim

3    ☐ sweet ☐ smile

4    ☐ snake ☐ stone

C Circle and say.

1 sm

2 sn
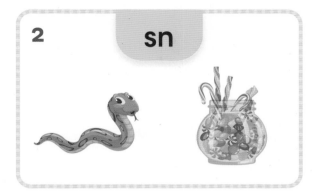

3 st
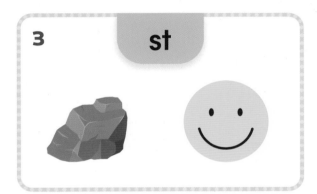

4 sw
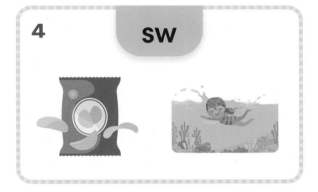

5 sn

6 st

7 sw
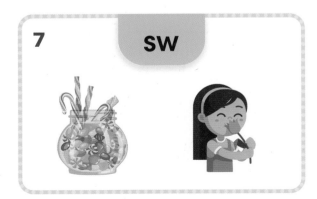

8 sm
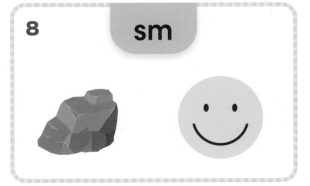

D Write the missing letters.

1

[ ][ ] ile

2
[ ][ ] one

3
[ ][ ] eet

4
[ ][ ] ake

5
[ ][ ] ell

6
[ ][ ] ove

7
[ ][ ] im

8
[ ][ ] ack

E Find and circle.

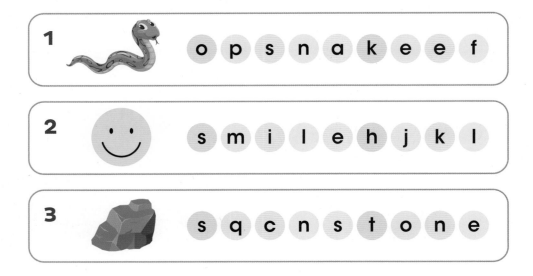

1 o p s n a k e e f

2 s m i l e h j k l

3 s q c n s t o n e

F Trace and write.

1  stove

2  sweet

3  smile

4  smell

5  snake

6  swim

7 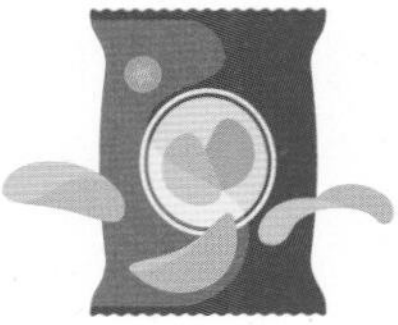 snack

8 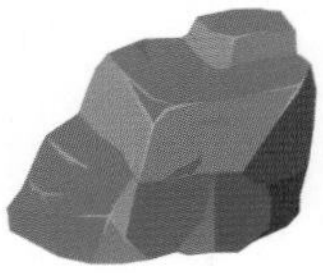 stone

A Say and match.

1 **ng**   2 **sh**   3 **th**   4 **ch**

B Check and write.

1    ☐ mouth ☐ shop

_____
- - - - - - - - - - - - - - -

2    ☐ cherry ☐ ring

_____
- - - - - - - - - - - - - - -

3   ☐ sing ☐ three

_____
- - - - - - - - - - - - - - -

4   ☐ fish ☐ lunch

_____
- - - - - - - - - - - - - - -

C Circle and say.

1 ch
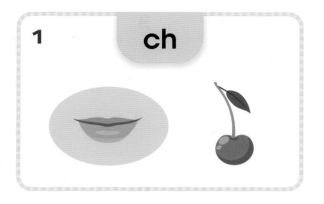

2 sh

3 th

4 ng
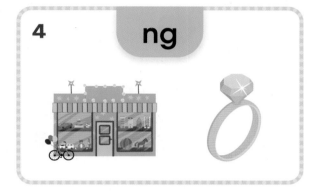

5 sh
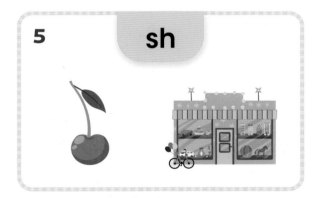

6 ng

7 ch
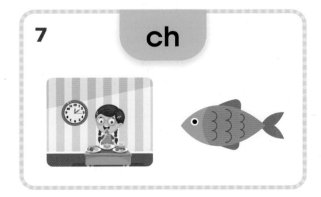

8 th
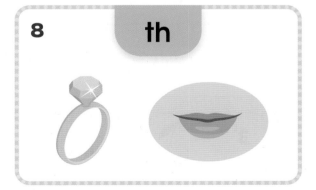

D Write the missing letters.

1

lun ☐ ☐

2

☐ ☐ ree

3

si ☐ ☐

4

☐ ☐ erry

5

fi ☐ ☐

6

mou ☐ ☐

7

☐ ☐ op

8

ri ☐ ☐

E Find and circle.

1 f g h a s i n g k

2 s h a m o u t h e

3 l i n c h e r r y

F **Trace and write.**

1 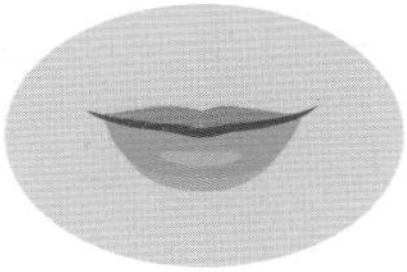   mouth _____ _____

2    sing _____ _____

3    lunch _____ _____

4    cherry _____ _____

5 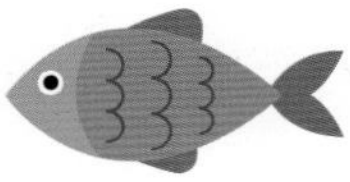   fish _____ _____

6    ring _____ _____

7    shop _____ _____

8    three _____ _____

A Say and circle.

1
fl   (gl)   bl

2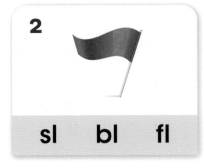
sl   bl   fl

3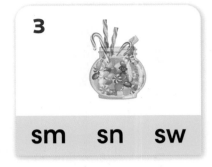
sm   sn   sw

4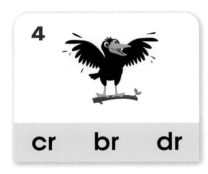
cr   br   dr

5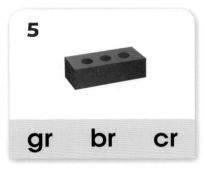
gr   br   cr

6
ch   sh   th

7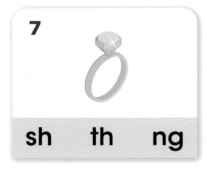
sh   th   ng

8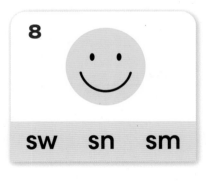
sw   sn   sm

9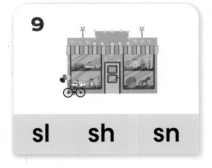
sl   sh   sn

10
br   bl   dr

11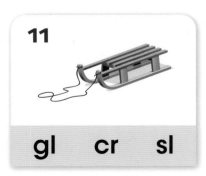
gl   cr   sl

12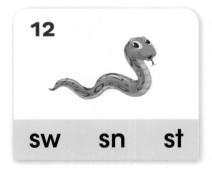
sw   sn   st

B Write the missing letters.

1
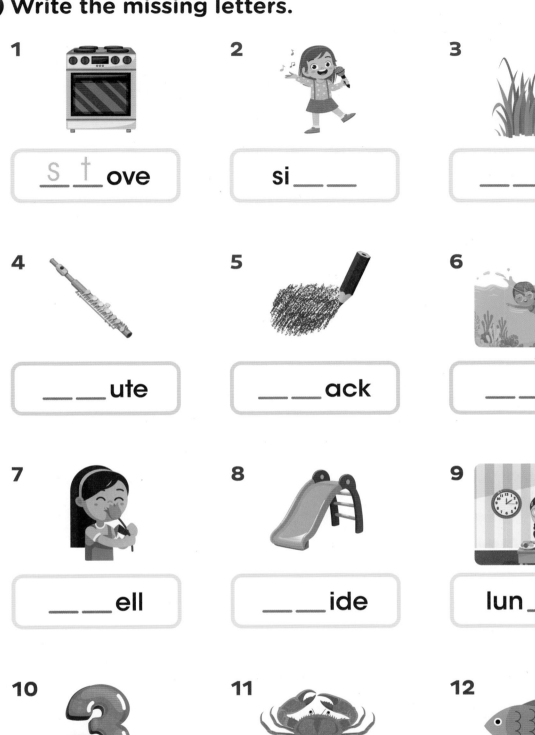
s t ___ove

2
si _____

3
___ass

4
___ute

5
___ack

6
___im

7
___ell

8
___ide

9
lun___

10
___ree

11
___ab

12
fi___

C Write the words.

1
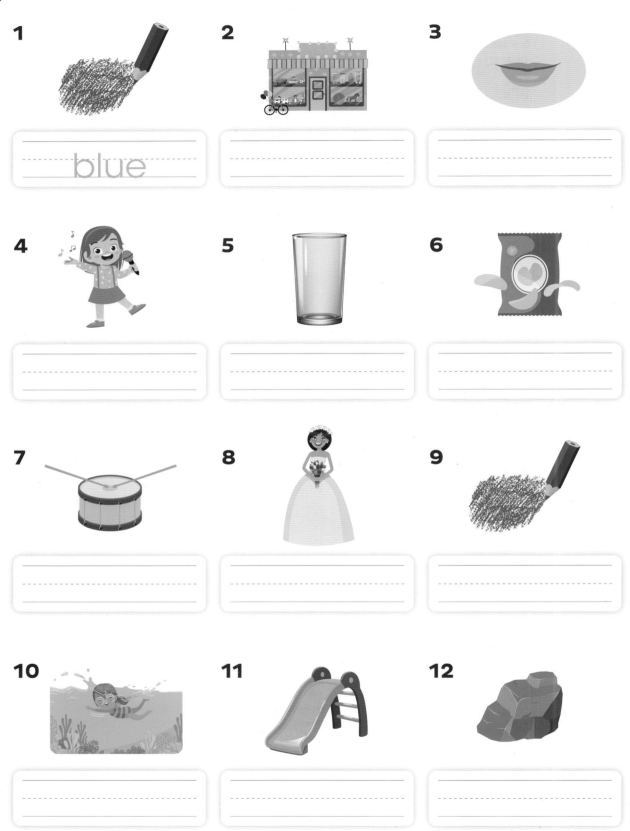
blue

2

3

4

5

6

7

8

9

10

11

12

D Read, choose, and write.

smell   brick   three   sled   green   cherry

1 A glove is on the ___sled___.

2 The _____ jam is in the shop.

3 Kate has _____ gloves.

4 The crab is on the _____.

5 The pup _____s the snack.

6 _____ rings are in the case.

A Say and match.

1 **oy**   2 **ay**   3 **oi**   4 **ai**

B Check and write.

1

☐ boil   ☐ play

2

☐ rain   ☐ boy

3

☐ coin   ☐ wait

4

☐ toy   ☐ gray

C Circle and say.

1 ai

2 ay

3 oi

4 oy

5 ay

6 oi

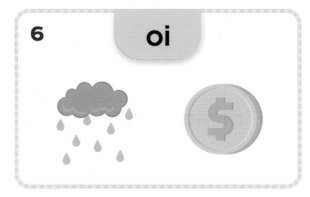

7 ai

8 oy

D Write the missing letters.

1 w ☐ ☐ t

2 b ☐ ☐ l

3 b ☐ ☐

4 r ☐ ☐ n

5 pl ☐ ☐

6 c ☐ ☐ n

7 gr ☐ ☐

8 t ☐ ☐

E Find and circle.

1 g c o i n i j k d

2 p h j k d p l a y

3 e r a i n c v b x

F Trace and write.

1  coin

2  boy

3  wait

4  rain

5  play

6  toy

7  gray

8  boil

UNIT 06   oa ow1 ou ow2

A Say and circle.

1

ou   ow

2
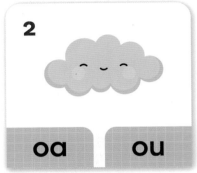
oa   ou

3

ow   oa

4

oa   ow

5
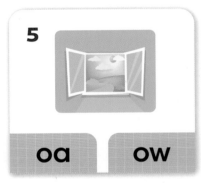
oa   ow

6
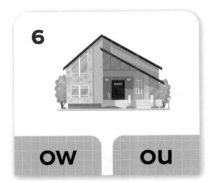
ow   ou

B Check and write.

1

☐ snow ☐ cloud
_____

2

☐ coat ☐ brown
_____

3

☐ cow ☐ house
_____

4

☐ goat ☐ window
_____

C Circle and say.

1 oa

2 ou

3 ow
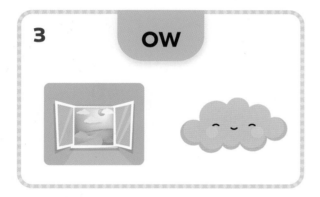

4 ow

5 ou

6 ow

7 oa

8 ow

D Write the missing letters.

1

br [ ][ ] n

2

g [ ][ ] t

3

c [ ][ ]

4

c [ ][ ] t

5

h [ ][ ] se

6

sn [ ][ ]

7

cl [ ][ ] d

8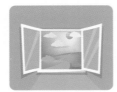

wind [ ][ ]

E Find and circle.

1   s i o q g o a t k

2   p b r o w n a x v

3   u r h o u s e t h

F Trace and write.

1. snow

2. house

3. cow

4. coat

5. window

6. brown

7. cloud

8. goat

A Say and match.

1 ir 2 or 3 er 4 ar

B Check and write.

1  ☐ shirt ☐ farmer
_____

2  ☐ car ☐ soccer
_____

3  ☐ girl ☐ corn
_____

4   ☐ horse ☐ singer
_____

C Circle and say.

1 ar

2 or

3 ir

4 er

5 or

6 ir

7 ar

8 er

D Write the missing letters.

1 f [ ] [ ] mer

2 sh [ ] [ ] t

3 socc [ ] [ ]

4 c [ ] [ ]

5 h [ ] [ ] se

6 g [ ] [ ] l

7 c [ ] [ ] n

8 sing [ ] [ ]

E Find and circle.

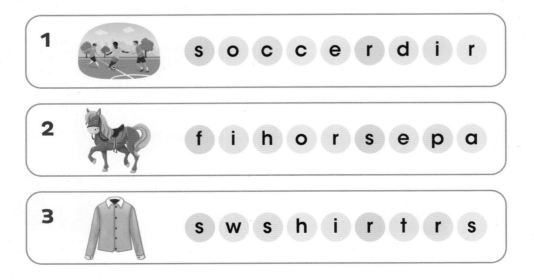

1 s o c c e r d i r

2 f i h o r s e p a

3 s w s h i r t r s

F Trace and write.

1. horse

2. singer

3. farmer

4. car

5. shirt

6. soccer

7. corn

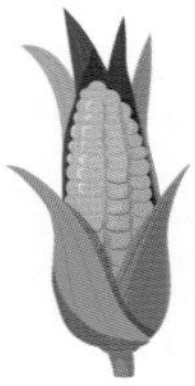

8. girl

Ⓐ Say and match.

1 long oo **2** ea **3** short oo **4** ee

Ⓑ Check and write.

1 ☐ book ☐ bee

2 ☐ meat ☐ moon

3 ☐ cook ☐ sea

4 ☐ pool ☐ tree

C Circle and say.

1 ee

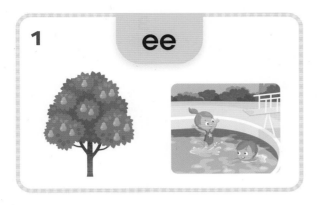

2 long oo

3 short oo

4 ea

5 ea

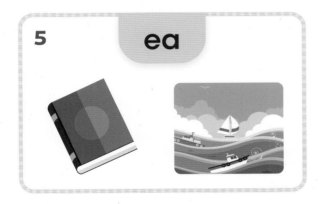

6 ee

7 long oo

8 short oo

D Write the missing letters.

1

b ▢ ▢

2

b ▢ ▢ k

3

m ▢ ▢ n

4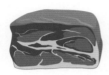

m ▢ ▢ t

5

tr ▢ ▢

6

c ▢ ▢ k

7

s ▢ ▢

8

p ▢ ▢ l

E Find and circle.

1  g h f e t c o o k

2 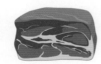 w n b m e a t f d

3   f e e b e e o f g

F Trace and write.

1 cook

2 pool

3 meat

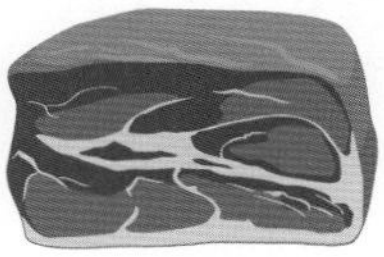

4 tree

5 sea

6 moon

7 bee

8 book

A Say and circle.

1

er   (ar)   or

2

oa   ou   ow

3

ay   oy   ai

4

ee   er   ea

5

oi   oy   ai

6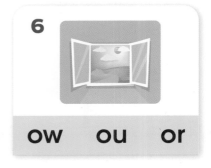

ow   ou   or

7

oi   oa   ow

8

er   ir   ar

9

or   ee   er

10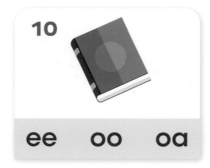

ee   oo   oa

11

ou   oo   ow

12

oy   oi   ou

B Write the missing letters.

1

tr e e

2

r____ ____ n

3

b____ ____

4

gr____ ____

5

br____ ____ n

6

g____ ____ l

7

sing____ ____

8

f____ ____ mer

9

p____ ____ l

10

m____ ____ t

11

cl____ ____ d

12

h____ ____ se

C Write the words.

1

play

2

3

4

5

6

7

8

9

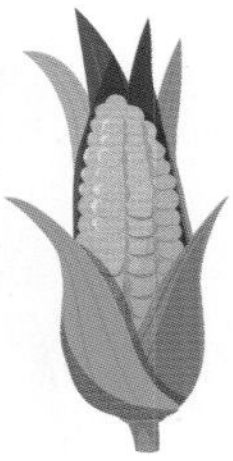

10

11

12

D **Read, choose, and write.**

pool   girl   brown   cloud   bee   soccer

1   I like my _____brown_____ coat.

2   A _____ sits on the book.

3   I see a big gray _____.

4   The _____ rides a horse.

5   The kids swim in the _____.

6   The girls play _____.

Oh! My Phonics

Oh! My Phonics is a four-level series of phonics books designed for EFL students to help them learn the fundamentals of phonics with efficient and practical methods. This series greatly assists young learners in understanding the relationship between letters and sounds effectively and adequately. *Oh! My Phonics* also introduces a number of common sight words embedded in fun phonics stories. In this way, children can naturally improve their sight word reading skills.

Oh! My Phonics Series

Alphabet Sounds **Short Vowels** **Long Vowels** **Double Letters**

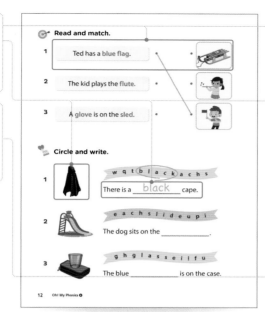

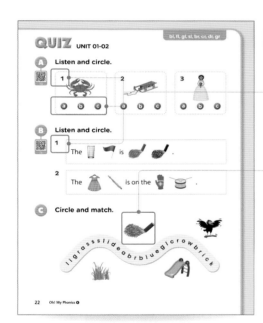

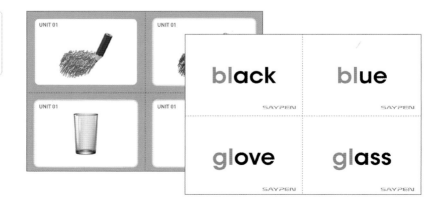

초등코치 천일문과
세이펜의 만남!

초등코치 천일문 시리즈 × 세이펜 학습의 장점

01	02	03	04	05
녹음기능을 활용하여 발음 교정 및 쉐도잉 학습 가능	112개 대표 패턴 및 모든 문장을 원어민 발음으로 실시간 재생	게임모드를 활용한 즐거운 영어학습 가능	Role play를 이용한 가상 대화 체험 (Sentence에 한함)	이해하기 어려운 문법적 내용을 쉬운 해설과 함께 바로듣기 가능 (Grammar에 한함)

* 〈초등코치 천일문 시리즈〉는 세이펜이 적용된 도서입니다.
　세이펜을 영어에 가져다 대기만 하면 원어민이 들려주는 생생한 영어 발음과 억양을 바로 확인할 수 있습니다.

* 세이펜은 본 교재에 포함되어 있지 않습니다. 기존에 보유하신 세이펜이 있다면 핀파일만 다운로드해서 바로 이용하실 수 있습니다.
　단, Role-Play 기능은 SBS-1000 이후 모델에서만 구동됩니다.